YOU'D *never* BELIEVE IT BUT...

snowflakes can fall in summer

and other facts about the seasons

Designed and produced by
Aladdin Books Ltd
28 Percy Street
London W1P 0LD

*First published in the United States
in 1998 by*
Copper Beech Books,
an imprint of
The Millbrook Press
2 Old New Milford Road
Brookfield, Connecticut 06804

Designed by
David West Children's Book Design
Computer illustrations
Stephen Sweet (Simon Girling & Associates)
Picture Research
Brooks Krikler Research
Project Editor
Sally Hewitt
Editors
Liz White and Sarah Levete

Library of Congress Cataloging-in-Publication Data
Taylor, Helen.
Snowflakes can fall in summer : and other facts
about seasons / by Helen Taylor : illustrated by
Stephen Sweet. p. cm. – (You'd never believe it but–)
Includes index. Summary: Explores the four seasons,
discussing such topics as the difference in shadows,
temperatures, and the length of days, and what
happens to plants and animals at different times of
the year. ISBN 0-7613-0815-6 (lib.bdg.)
    1. Seasons–Juvenile literature. [1. Seasons.]
I. Sweet, Stephen, 1965- ill. II. Title. III. Series.
QB637.4.T39 1998   97-51777
508.2–dc21   CIP   AC

YOU'D *never* BELIEVE IT BUT... snowflakes can fall in summer

and other facts about the seasons

Helen Taylor

COPPER BEECH BOOKS
BROOKFIELD, CONNECTICUT

Contents

Introduction

Have you ever wondered why lambs are born in the spring or why some animals hide away in the cold months?

A season is a change in the pattern of the weather. The seasons — spring, summer, fall, and winter — bring lots of changes to nature.

Join Jack and Jo as they discover some fantastic facts about the seasons.

FUN PROJECTS Wherever you see this sign, it means that there is a project that you can do.

Each project will help you to understand more about the subject. You'd never believe it but… each project is fun to do.

A year

Did you know that Earth, the planet we live on, is a ball of rock? Did you know that the sun is an enormous ball of fire? The sun gives us all our heat and light. Nothing on Earth could live and grow without sunlight.

The earth and the sun are not shown to scale in this diagram.

In many parts of the world, the year is divided into four seasons — spring, summer, fall, and winter. As the earth moves around the sun, the seasons change, bringing different kinds of weather.

The earth never stops moving around the sun. It takes 365 days, which is a whole year, for the earth to move all the way around the sun.

Summer

Winter

Sun

Earth

Places getting the most heat and light are having their summer while other places are having their winter.

You'd never believe it but...

You are traveling through space at 67,000 miles per hour! This is the speed at which the earth travels around the sun.

Winter

Summer

Can you see that the earth is not upright? It is tilted so that one half is closer to the sun than the other. The other half gets closer as the earth moves around the sun.

MAKE SUMMER AND WINTER
1. Use a ball as the earth and a flashlight as the sun.
2. With a friend, put a piece of colored cellophane around the middle of the ball.
3. Write your name on some cellophane above this line. Write your friend's name on some cellophane below this line.
4. In the dark, tilt one name toward the flashlight. Shine the flashlight on the ball.

It's winter where I am.

My half of the earth is the brightest. It's summer where I am.

Jack
Jo

Night and...

The earth isn't only moving around the sun, it is spinning too. It takes 24 hours to spin around once. We call this a day.

When our part of Earth is facing the sun, it is daytime. When our part of Earth is facing away from the sun, it is nighttime.

At night, people often stay in their homes and most animals go to sleep. Nights are longer in the winter.

day

You'd never believe it but...

Your shadow is longer in the winter and shorter in the summer!

SHADOW PATTERNS

1. In the morning, stand outside. Ask a friend to draw around your shadow with a piece of chalk.
2. Go back to the same place at lunchtime. Ask your friend to draw around your shadow again.
3. Do the same in the afternoon. What has happened to your shadow?

We can see the sun in different places in the sky during the day. It looks like the sun is moving, but really the earth is spinning around the sun.

Look, Jo, your shadow is the same shape as you.

The sun can't shine through me!

Daytime is when you go to school and play outside. Days are longer in the summer.

All over the world

The equator is an imaginary line around the middle of the earth. It divides the earth in half. We call the top half the Northern Hemisphere, and we call the bottom half the Southern Hemisphere.

High up in the sky, the sun is almost directly above the equator. This makes it hot there all year round.

People who live near the equator wear light clothes to keep cool.

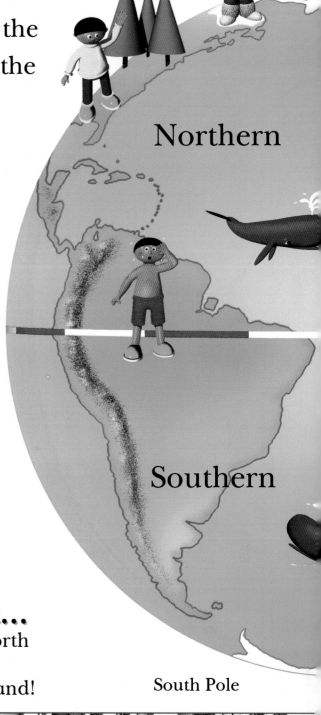

Northern

Southern

South Pole

You'd never believe it but...
It is always winter on Christmas day in North America — but it is always summer on Christmas day in Australia and New Zealand!

North Pole

Parts of the world on either side of the equator have four seasons — spring, summer, fall, and winter.

Hemisphere

Equator

Hemisphere

Gigantic icebergs from near the North Pole float south where they melt in the warmer waters.

MELTING ICE
Have you noticed that ice cubes stay frozen in your freezer?
Watch them melt when you leave them out in a warm room.

Are there any icebergs near the equator?

No. The equator is too hot for icebergs. They would melt, like my ice cubes!

At the North and South Poles, the sun is low in the sky. This makes it cold all year round. Animals have thick coats and extra layers of fat.

Spring

Spring is the season when lots of changes take place. The weather gets warmer after the cold winter and the days begin to get longer. Look out for new buds on the trees. Can you see shoots beginning to push through the ground?

There is often bright sunshine after a heavy rain shower. You may be able to see a rainbow in the sky.

Let's see who can make the biggest splash.

Quick, before the sun dries up the puddles!

Spring is a good time for baby animals to be born. The weather is warm and there is plenty of food for them to eat.

You'd never believe it but...

The ostrich, the biggest bird in the world, lays eggs as big as your head!

Ostrich egg

Chicken egg

In the spring, birds lay their eggs and baby birds hatch out.

Spring flowers open and yards become colorful again.

OPENING BUDS
1. Put a daffodil bud into water. Watch it slowly open out into a flower.
2. Add some red food coloring to the water.
What happens to the yellow daffodil?

Summer

Summer comes after spring. It is the hottest season of the year. The days are longer. The sun feels hottest when it is high in the sky at midday.

There are lots of creatures around in the summer. Look out for them visiting flowers or resting in cool places in the shade.

Listen! These insects are buzzing.

I've found a silver trail. I think this snail made it.

You'd never believe it but...

Snowflakes can fall in summer! They land on cold mountain tops, but melt in warm air on lower ground.

When it is hot you often feel sticky and sweaty. Did you know that drops of sweat on your skin actually help you to keep cool?

What can you do to keep cool on a hot day?

FLOWER SANDWICHES
1. Pick some flowers and place them on paper towels. Try not to put one flower on top of another flower.
2. Now, put more paper towels on top to make a flower sandwich.
3. Put your flower sandwich between the pages of a thick, heavy book. Shut the book and leave it for two weeks.
4. After two weeks, the flowers will have dried out. Now you can put them on colored paper.
5. Cover them with ConTact paper to make them into a picture.

Fall

Fall comes between summer and winter. The weather starts to get colder and windier. The mornings and evenings are often misty.

You may find it hard to get out of bed because it is darker when you wake up.

Green leaves from some trees turn gold, orange, and red. They fall off the branches. During the winter, they will rot in the ground.

I think this leaf is from a maple tree.

The leaves are all crispy and crunchy.

You'd never believe it but...

Collect some fall leaves. You can tell by their shape what tree they come from.

Some trees grow needles! They are really long, thin leaves that can survive very cold winters. They stay on the trees all year round.

LEAF PRINTS

1. Put a leaf on some newspaper. Paint it with the colors of a fall leaf.

2. Put the leaf, paint side upward, onto clean newspaper. Press some plain paper on top of it.

3. Peel the leaf off carefully. When the paint dries, cut out your leaf print.

In the fall, there are lots of seeds, nuts, and berries ready to be eaten. Birds and animals have plenty to eat in the fall, but there will not be so much food for them when the winter comes.

Acorn

Sycamore seed

Horse chestnut

Winter

Winter is the coldest season of the year. The days are very short and the nights are long.

It's fun to play outside in the winter, but you need to dress warmly. What do you like to do outside in winter?

Frost often covers the ground on winter mornings. There may even be some snow. Look out for tracks left by birds and animals. Who do you think they belong to?

You'd never believe it but...

Shivering helps you to keep warm. When you shiver you make lots of little movements. These movements create heat energy in your body that helps you to warm up.

When it is cold you can see your breath. Warm breath looks like steam in the cold air.

I think that a bird made these prints.

MAKE A SNOWFLAKE

1. Cut out a paper circle.
2. Fold it in half.
3. Fold the ends over.
4. Fold it in half again. Along the right edge, as shown, cut out a shape. Follow the line in the diagram.
5. Open it up!

Wet and dry

There are places near the equator that only have two seasons — the wet season and the dry season.

The wet season brings violent storms called monsoons. Monsoon rain can be so heavy that houses and cars are washed away and roads just disappear. There are often fierce thunderstorms with dangerous flashes of lightning.

You can count the seconds between a flash of lightning and a roll of thunder to tell whether a storm is close or far away.

Even when the monsoon rain stops, it can still feel hot and sticky. People find it hard to keep their houses dry and comfortable.

DRY SOIL

What happens to soil in the hot sunshine?

1. Collect some damp soil from the park or your yard.
2. Weigh it on a scale.
3. Ask an adult to put it in a medium hot oven on a cookie sheet for half an hour.
4. Now weigh it again.

Do you think plants will be able to grow in this soil?

Rivers and lakes begin to shrink during the dry season. Animals have to search for water to drink. The hot sunshine makes the soil very dry and dusty.

You'd never believe it but...

Rice grows underwater, so it grows very well in places that have a wet season.

Migration

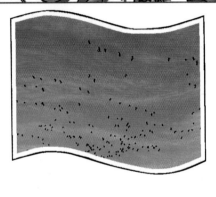

Birds who live in the Northern Hemisphere eat seeds, berries, insects, and other creatures such as worms and snails. There is plenty for them to eat in spring and summer.

But at the end of summer, you can see birds flocking together on rooftops and telephone wires. They are getting ready to fly away from the winter to find the summer on the other side of the world.

The long journey that birds make to look for food is called migration.

You'd never believe it but...
The Arctic tern flies 12,000 miles from the Arctic near the North Pole to the Antarctic near the South Pole.

Not all birds migrate. Some, such as sparrows, stay through the winter.

Winter is a good time to put out food for birds because there is less for them to eat. Don't forget to put water out for the birds, too.

Where shall we put the bird cake?

Not near the window. The people inside might scare the birds away.

BIRD CAKE

Ask an adult to help you make this bird cake.

1. Make bread crumbs out of a stale loaf of bread. Mix in raw peanuts and chopped up bacon.

2. Melt some butter in a pan. Pour it over the mixture. Stir it and leave it to cool. Put the bird cake outside for the birds to eat.

Hibernation

When the days begin to get shorter, animals know it is time to get ready for winter.

Squirrels, chipmunks, and bears fatten themselves up while there is still plenty of food around. Bears hide away in caves. Squirrels and chipmunks (*left*) huddle in their nests.

Now it is time for them to fall into a deep sleep called hibernation.

While animals are hibernating, they don't use up much energy so they don't need to eat.

They become very cold. Their hearts beat slowly and they only breathe a few times each minute.

Food gives you the energy you need to keep warm and active.

You'd never believe it but...

Animals that hibernate sleep all winter. They are woken up by the arrival of the warmer spring weather.

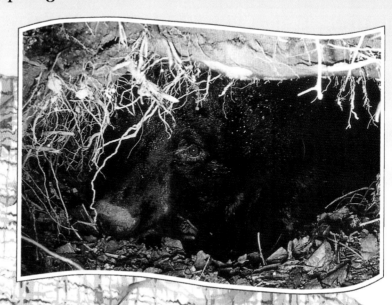

Phew! I'm out of breath and my heart's beating fast!

Take a rest! My heart isn't beating fast.

USING ENERGY

1. Notice how slowly or quickly you are breathing. Feel your heart beating by finding your pulse in your wrist like this.

2. Now do something energetic for a few minutes, like running.

What happens to your breathing and your heartbeat? Does running make you feel hungry?

Harvest

Harvest usually comes at the end of the summer. It is a very busy time of the year for farmers. The crops they planted in spring are ready to be picked and used.

Some fields of wheat are so big that they stretch as far as you can see. Giant machines called combines work all day harvesting the wheat.

Look at all that wheat. I wonder what they'll use it for.

You'd never believe it but...

Soil needs a good rest. After the harvest, farmers plow their fields and let the soil rest during winter. It will be ready for new crops to be planted in the spring.

They will make it into flour for bread.

Does your country have a festival to celebrate harvest? A good harvest means there will be plenty to eat.

The crops farmers grow depend on the kinds of weather they have in their part of the world. Sugarcane, cotton, and pineapples all need very hot weather to ripen.

Hot and steamy

In the rain forests that grow near the equator there is no spring, summer, fall, or winter.

It is hot, wet, and steamy all year round.

Go into the bathroom after someone has taken a hot bath or shower. The air feels hot and steamy, much like the air in a rain forest.

Some trees in the rain forest grow huge leaves. These leaves help to form a canopy, like a giant umbrella.

It shelters the ground below from the sunshine and rain.

It's too hot to wear a sweater in here!

Brightly colored birds, monkeys, frogs, snakes, and butterflies are just some of the creatures that make their home in the canopy.

All kinds of plants grow high on the tree trunks closer to the sunlight.

Look, I can draw a picture in the steam on the mirror.

You'd never believe it but...

Rain collects in the petals of huge flowers called bromeliads. These pools of rainwater are big enough for frogs to swim in and lay their eggs.

Most plants need lots of sunlight to grow. Only ferns and mosses grow on the shady forest floor.

Glossary

Energy
Food and sunlight give animals and people the energy that they need to move around, grow, and keep warm.

Equator
The equator is an imaginary line around the middle of the earth that you cannot see. Along the equator, it is hot all year round.

Frost
Frost is formed in cold weather when tiny droplets of water freeze on the ground, on plants, and on windows.

Hemisphere
The equator divides the earth into two halves called hemispheres. The top half is called the Northern Hemisphere and the bottom half is called the Southern Hemisphere.

Hibernation
When it is cold and difficult to find food in the winter, some animals go to sleep to save energy. This long, deep sleep is called hibernation.

Lightning
Lightning is a flash of light in the sky. It is caused by the electricity in a thunderstorm. Lightning can cause damage to objects and injury to people.

Migration
Migration is the name for the long journey that some birds and animals make to look for food.

Monsoon
Parts of the world with only wet and dry seasons have monsoons. These are violent storms with very heavy rainfall.

Planet

A planet is a huge ball of rock in space that has no heat or light of its own. Our planet, Earth, is one of nine planets that move around the sun.

Pole

The North Pole and the South Pole are imaginary points at opposite ends of the earth. At the North and South Poles it is freezing cold all year round.

Rainbow

When sunlight shines through raindrops, it splits into seven colors. A rainbow is the great arc of colors that you can see in the sky when there is sunshine and rain together.

Season

A season is a change in the pattern of the weather that brings changes to nature. Many parts of the world on either side of the equator have four seasons — spring, summer, fall, and winter. Other parts of the world closer to the equator have only two seasons — wet and dry.

Shadow

Rays of sunlight cannot shine through solid objects. When the sun shines on you, your body makes a dark shape where the sun cannot shine. This shape is called a shadow.

Thunderstorm

A thunderstorm occurs when electricity in huge, dark clouds causes flashes of lightning and crashes of thunder.

Weather

When we ask "What is the weather like today?," we mean "what is it like outside?" Is it hot or cold? Is it sunny, cloudy, windy, or is it raining?

Year

It takes a year for the earth to move all the way around the sun. There are 365 days in a year.

Index

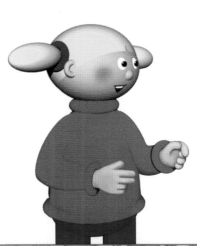

PHOTO CREDITS
Abbreviations: t-top, m-middle, b-bottom, r-right, l-left, c-centre.

All the pictures in this book were supplied by Roger Vlitos except the following pages: 10br, 11, 12, 13mr & 21tl - Frank Spooner Pictures. 15tr, 21bl & br, 22b & 27b - Spectrum Color Library. 24 & 25tr - Bruce Coleman Collection.